DESIGNS AND PATTERNS
FROM HISTORIC ORNAMENT

Formerly titled
OUTLINES OF ORNAMENT IN THE LEADING STYLES

BY W. & G. AUDSLEY

DOVER PUBLICATIONS, INC.
NEW YORK

Published in Canada by General Publishing Company, Ltd., 31 Lesmill Road, Don Mills, Toronto, Ontario.

Published in the United Kingdom by Constable and Company, Ltd., 10 Orange Street, London WC2H 7EG.

This Dover edition, first published in 1968, is an unabridged republication of the work originally published by Scribner and Welford in 1882 under the title *Outlines of Ornament in the Leading Styles*. A new list of plates has been prepared especially for this Dover edition.

DOVER *Pictorial Archive* SERIES

International Standard Book Number: 0-486-21931-3
Library of Congress Catalog Card Number: 68-19174

Manufactured in the United States of America

Dover Publications, Inc.
31 East 2nd Street
Mineola, N.Y. 11501

PREFACE

NOTWITHSTANDING the numerous and important Works on Ornament which have been published in this and other countries, during the last twenty years, we feel assured that there is still room for the more humble Work which we now lay before the public, differing as it does in aim and treatment from any that have preceded it. In this direction probably Works of such magnitude and elaboration as Owen Jones' *Grammar of Ornament*, and Racinet's *L'Ornement Polychrome* will not be again produced in our day. They give superb collections of Decorative and Ornamental Designs, grouped under the respective Nations or Schools which have produced them, and supply the Decorative Artist and Ornamentist with an almost inexhaustible fount of inspiration; and in their special subjects, are Works of the highest historical and archæological value. If they fail in anything, it is in their purely educational aspect; that is to say, they do not—by grouping ornaments together which are similar in their motives and general treatment, and are the productions of the different National Schools of Art in different ages— bring directly and clearly before the eye of the student the true scope of each species of ornamental design, and distinctly impress him with its principles of construction, and point out how those principles have been modified or developed by different artists, and at different epochs of art. An example may assist our meaning here:—The Fret, for instance, is an ornament very commonly believed to belong exclusively to Greek Art, and in most works on ornament it is confined to that school, but by looking over a collection of Greek Frets, the student can gather partial information only regarding the subject of Fret ornamentation, and he is not made aware of the fact that the Greeks were not the first or only people who used it. Before the student of art can arrive at a clear and satisfactory knowledge of the subject, he must be supplied with examples selected from all quarters; and his attention must be directed to the numerous types and forms this species of ornament assumes in the Art Works of all those nations who have adopted it to any important extent.

It is with the hope of doing good service, in this direction, to the cause of Art Education, that our present Work is produced; and instead of grouping our illustrations, as is usually done, under the heads of Greek, Roman, Moresque, Gothic, &c., we have classified them, according to their motives, under such heads as Fret Ornament, Interlaced Ornament, Diaper Ornament, &c. The student will thus have an opportunity of fairly realising what has been done by ancient and modern artists all over the world in the different classes of ornament; he will, in short, be able to obtain OUTLINES of each, upon which he can base his own inventions or developments. We give short and concise remarks, describing the ornaments, and pointing out the motives and leading principles observed by their respective designers.

We have, in addition, to point out that in our Work we deal with FORM alone, divested of the fascination of gold and colour, and we feel that we do wisely in this, for the first education of the ornamentist must be in form; let him master the elements of beauty and fitness in that, and the addition of colour becomes an easy matter. Were this fact more commonly realised, we should at the present time have more good, and less meaningless and crude, decoration than we see around us.

We have selected the title, "OUTLINES OF ORNAMENT," with a double intention: first to express that our Work is so arranged that the constructive outlines of certain classes of ornament can readily be obtained by the study of its plates; second, to express that FORM alone has been adopted as the characteristic of its illustrations, and that they are accordingly in outline, and without the body imparted by the filling in with colour.

The entire series of Plates is produced by Photo-lithography, from drawings specially prepared for the Work by ourselves and pupils. They are drawn to a large scale, so as to be decidedly practical and clear. Though certain of the necessary links in the series of illustrations have appeared elsewhere in a different form, the bulk of the drawings are from original sources; some reproduced from tracings made by ourselves from the walls, columns, or other portions of buildings, as in the case of those designs from the Church of Notre Dame de Bonsecours, at Rouen, and the Abbey of Saint Denis; and others from works of art in our own and other collections, as in the case of those of Japanese origin.

A good series of Japanese Art designs has of late been much sought after by decorative artists, on account of their peculiarly suggestive character; in the present Work, therefore, we give a collection of such patterns as properly group themselves under the classes of ornament we illustrate, selected chiefly on account of their suitability for every-day use by the ornamentist.

It is our desire to make the Work eminently practical in its nature. The illustrations are selected on account of their useful and suggestive character, to act as every-day helps to the designer and decorator, in the composition of enrichments and decorations for all purposes. It is for this reason that we have chosen the examples both from ancient and modern sources; the modern supplying illustrations of certain classes of decoration which are not found in the ancient, or are at best indifferently represented.

All designs which are coloured in the originals in any decided manner, have their systems of colouring marked for reference.

With this brief explanation of the nature and aims of our Work, we submit it to the consideration of all Students of Art.

W. & G. AUDSLEY.

Liverpool, 1881.

LIST OF PLATES

PLATE

FRET ORNAMENT

Egyptian and Classic 1
Classic [A] 2
Middle Age [A] 3
Oriental [A] 4

FRET DIAPER ORNAMENT

Japanese 5

INTERLACED ORNAMENT

Celtic 6
Celtic [B] 7
Arabian 8
Moresque 9
Moresque [B] 10
Middle Age [A] 11
Russian Middle Age 12

POWDERED DIAPER ORNAMENT

Japanese 13

POWDERED ORNAMENT

Modern French 14
Japanese [A] 15
Japanese [B] 16
Japanese [C] 17

DIAPER ORNAMENT

Egyptian [A] 18
Egyptian [B] 19
Arabian 20
Moresque 21
Persian [A] 22
Persian [B] 23
Japanese [A] 24
Japanese [B] 25
Japanese [C] 26

PLATE

DIAPER ORNAMENT (*Continued*)

Japanese [D] 27
Japanese [E] 28
English Middle Age [A] 29
Sicilian [A] 30
Dutch Middle Age [A] 31
Dutch Middle Age [A*] 32
Dutch Middle Age [B] 33
Dutch Middle Age [C] 34
Modern French [A] 35
Modern French [B] 36
Modern French [B*] 37
Modern French [C] 38
Modern French [D] 39
Modern French [E] 40
Modern French [F] 41
Modern French [G] 42
German Middle Age [A] 43
Middle Age [D] 44
Middle Age [E] 45
Middle Age [F] 46
Middle Age [G] 47
Middle Age [H] 48
Chinese 49

CONVENTIONAL FOLIAGE

Middle Age [A] 50
Middle Age [B] 51
Middle Age [C] 52
Modern French [A] 53
Modern French [B] 54
Modern French [C] 55
Modern French [D] 56
Persian 57
Greek [A] 58
Greek [B] 59
Japanese 60

FRET ORNAMENT

BY what race of artists Fret Ornament was first introduced is not known, and it is more than probable that it will remain an unanswered question for all time. We do know, however, that it existed in its simpler forms in the earliest epochs of art; and, as few combinations of straight lines could be made without accidentally forming something resembling a fret, it would be a matter of surprise if we did not find it appearing in the decorative works of every artistic people.

The following diagrams (Fig. 1), showing the simple and obvious arrangements of pieces of wood of one size, or bricks placed on edge, such as might be made by an

1

intelligent child at play, contain the first ideas of Fret Ornament, and, indeed, the germs of its most complex development.

In early Egyptian hieroglyphics we find two phonographic characters which are component parts of frets (Figs. 2 and 3). With several of these combined in order,

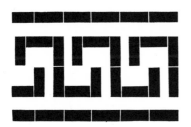

2

3

certain varieties of frets may readily be constructed, as in the diagrams below (Fig. 4); and it is worthy of note that by a simple repetition of an entwined combination of two

4

characters, in the form of Fig. 3, the Egyptian fret is produced which we illustrate on our first Plate of FRET ORNAMENT, EGYPTIAN AND CLASSIC, Fig. 1. This is from a drawing, made by our friend Mr. R. PHENE SPIERS, from a painted ceiling of a tomb at Siout.

The Egyptians were unquestionably a mixed race; a large portion of which, there is sufficient authority for believing, originally came from Tartary or India. To this portion is attributed the introduction of the art of writing. It is just possible, therefore, that the fret characters may have originated in the East long before they were used by the Egyptians. But it is quite unnecessary to carry speculation further in a Work simply dedicated to FORM, as this is.

Our next step is to Greek Art, where we find the fret to have been used from the archaic period, as a favourite enrichment on painted vases; and it is to these works, and others which were fabricated by the Etruscans, a Greek colony which settled in that part of Italy now called Tuscany, that we are indebted for the rich series of Fret Ornaments now at our disposal. The Greek fret, *par excellence*, is that represented in

5

Fig. 5, where it will be observed the meander is single, continuous, and in all parts exactly the same width as the spaces it leaves in its course. This fret, and indeed every one found throughout Greek art, can be readily constructed by filling up certain contiguous squares on reticulated paper—that is, paper marked with lines crossing at right angles and at equal distances from each other. To delineate Classic frets with facility, it is advisable for the student to reticulate the surface upon which he is to work: it is the only method to secure a perfect result. Certain other varieties of frets, as we shall shortly show, require a different mode of procedure. To draw the fret on Plate CLASSIC [A], Fig. 2, one set of lines has to cross the other at the desired angle. An example of a reticulated surface filled in with fret-work is supplied by the labyrinth, illustrated on Plate MIDDLE AGE [A], Fig. 1.

The Greek artists, in designing their frets, always endeavoured, however complicated the pattern might be, to keep the meanders continuous; and in this respect differed from both the Egyptian and Oriental designers, who appear to have considered the continuous treatment an unnecessary element of beauty.

The fret did not undergo any material modification in the hands of the Roman artists; unless we can attribute to them the introduction into decorative art of the class frequently met with in their mosaic pavements, of which Fig. 1 on Plate CLASSIC [A] is an example. This is from a mosaic found at Pompeii; and the design is of such a nature as to admit of endless repetition over a surface.

In early and mediæval Christian Art the fret is frequently met with. In Romanesque architecture it is a characteristic ornament, and it assumes forms directly derived from ancient Roman work; and in the decorative art of the period it also occurs, some-times under more original treatments, as in the wall painting in the Church of Tournus (Saône-et-Loire), represented in Plate MIDDLE AGE [A], Fig. 6. Figs. 3, 4, 9 and

10 are from Celtic manuscripts dating between the seventh and ninth centuries; and Figs. 7 and 8 are from a French manuscript of the twelfth century. The centre square of this Plate is from a labyrinth in the Church of St. Bertin, at St. Omer, and Fig. 2 is from an embroidered maniple, both works of the early years of the thirteenth century.

Probably no artists have displayed greater appreciation of Fret decoration than the Japanese, though it is highly probable that they were much later in adopting it than the Chinese. There is little real difference between the ornament as presented in the works of these two nations; but it is much more largely used by the Japanese, both for border and surface decoration. In some examples the Oriental frets resemble those of the Classic artists; for instance, compare Fig. 11, on Plate ORIENTAL [A] with Fig. 5, on Plate CLASSIC [A]: it will be observed that the white pattern of the former and the black of the latter are practically the same, the Oriental example simply being lengthened in treatment. The chief peculiarity of Oriental frets lies in their being discontinuous, or compiled without the view of carrying the eye uninterruptedly onward in their meanders; but examples are sometimes met with which are quite as perfect in their continuity as the Greek frets. We give three notable instances in Figs. 2, 5, and 13, on Plate ORIENTAL [A]. All the other patterns on this Plate show interrupted or discontinuous frets. Discontinuous frets are comparatively rare in Classic art, but we are able to give representative examples in Figs. 2, 3, and 6, on Plate EGYPTIAN AND CLASSIC; and Fig. 8, on Plate CLASSIC [A]. In middle age art the continuous fret was most commonly used, but interrupted frets are sometimes met with, as in Fig. 3, Plate MIDDLE AGE [A].

FRET DIAPER ORNAMENT

In ancient Egyptian and Classic times, the Fret was occasionally extended so as to cover a surface, after the fashion of a diaper, examples of which treatment are given on Plate FRET ORNAMENT, EGYPTIAN AND CLASSIC, and in Fig. 1 Plate FRET ORNAMENT, CLASSIC [A]. Diapers based on the Fret, but with curved lines instead of angular, are frequently met with in Egyptian work; examples are given in Fig. 4 on Plate DIAPER ORNAMENT, EGYPTIAN [B], and the two upper patterns on Plate DIAPER ORNAMENT, EGYPTIAN [A]. In Celtic work we also find Fret diapers, as on a fragment of a stone cross found at the church of Penally, near Tenby. This fragment displayed a diaper almost identical with the second Egyptian pattern given on the last-mentioned Plate, the curves being rather more stiff, in the manner usual in Celtic ornament. The Japanese are very fond of Fret diapers, and display much skill in their arrangement. The four given on Plate FRET DIAPER ORNAMENT, JAPANESE, are representative examples. An Arabian variety of Fret diaper is given in Fig. 3, on Plate DIAPER ORNAMENT, ARABIAN.

INTERLACED ORNAMENT

WE may safely class Interlaced Ornament among the most primitive styles of decoration. The natural interweaving of the branches of trees, or the artificial plaiting of twigs or osiers, in the formation of rude huts or baskets, would be sufficient to suggest, and very probably did first suggest, the formation of interlaced ornamentation. Our friend, the late Mr. Gilbert J. French, in an interesting tract, entitled "*An attempt to explain the origin and meaning of the early Interlaced Ornamentation found on the Ancient Sculptured Stones of Scotland, Ireland, and the Isle of Man,*" expresses his decided opinion that the interlaced work, commonly designated Runic or Celtic, had its origin in interlaced twigs or basket-work.

As Mr. French's brochure was printed for private circulation only, we need not apologise for giving some quotations from it here. He says :—

" Any reasonable and honest attempt to explain the origin of the singularly elegant interlaced ornamentation, familiar to archæologists as the very earliest style of artistic decoration known in the British islands, must be entitled to favourable consideration. The style of interlaced ornament to which I refer is found in an infinite variety of devices on the earliest sculpture, whether of stone or metal, and in the oldest manuscripts and illuminations of Britain and Ireland. It retained its peculiar distinctive character throughout the Roman occupation of Britain, slightly modified by, and often mixed with, classical ornaments. These, however, in a great measure disappeared during the Saxon period, a circumstance which induces the belief that, whatever its origin and purpose, interlaced ornamentation was equally familiar to the Saxon invaders and to the British aborigines. It entered largely into Norman architecture ; but from the time of the Conquest it gradually became less used, though traces of it are to be met with at nearly every period in the history of British art. . .

" The aborigines of this or any other country of corresponding climate, after discovering some natural cave, or making for themselves a rude hut, would probably take their next step in constructive art by attempting to form such utensils as might contain, and enable them to preserve, the fruits and seeds necessary for food. Assuming that they were then unprovided with even the rudest tools—for we refer to a time before our far-off ancestors knew the use of bronze or iron,—they would form these utensils by twisting together the long, pliant osiers with which the land abounded, and of which, by the unaided action of the fingers, they could form baskets excellently adapted for the required purpose. No other branch of art is even now so independent of tools, and none has been so universally diffused or so long and uninterruptedly practised as basket-making. It is the humble parent of all textile art, the most elaborate tissues produced by the loom or the needle being but progressive developments proceeding from the rude wattle-work of unclothed savages. Basket-making is the first natural step in the path of civilization. To this day the earliest effort of infantile ingenuity among the rural population is directed to making (as it were by intuitive instinct) personal ornaments of plaited rushes, and that, too, in patterns some of which are identical with the devices engraved by our pre-historic ancestors on their old sculptured stones. . .

"A manufacture which was probably progressing for many centuries before the Romans invaded Britain, must necessarily have acquired a certain amount of refined ornament as a result of so much experience and practice. We have, indeed, direct evidence that the Romans greatly admired the ornamental baskets of the British, which were exported in large quantities to Rome."

After continuing at some length on this branch of his subject, and alluding to the possibility of vessels of clay being moulded inside baskets, and the fact that the earliest specimens of British pottery bear a rude decoration, closely resembling the indentations which would be left by a basket-work mould, he turns his attention directly to the chief subject of his paper.

"It was the custom of those earnest and indefatigable men" (the first Christian missionaries in Britain and Ireland) "to place crosses in every place where they succeeded in making converts, or in which they planted a church, chapel, or monastery; and it becomes a question of some interest to ascertain the materials of these early symbols of the Christian faith, which must have been extensively spread over the land. Clearly they were not of stone, since we know that even after the Romans left England the natives had not sufficient skill to build a wall of that material; nor have we any reason to believe that they had the ability or the tools requisite for the construction of a cross of timber, which would demand the use of cutting instruments with finer edges than those necessary for stone. Under these circumstances it is only natural that the British convert would dedicate to the glory of God the products of that talent which had acquired for him a continental celebrity. The basket-work, so prized at Rome, was the most valuable oblation that the pious ancient Briton could offer to the services of his new religion, and thus it was that the first emblems of Christianity erected in England were (almost necessarily) constructed of basket-work.

"The perishable nature of the materials forbids us to expect almost any other than inferential evidence that crosses of basket-work ever existed, but happily this is not denied to us. A careful examination of the admirable engravings of the sculptured stones of Scotland, the ancient Irish crosses, and the curious monumental remains of the Isle of Man, together with many existing carved crosses in England and Wales, cannot fail to convince any unprejudiced observer that the beautiful interlaced ornamentation so lavishly employed on these sculptures derived its origin from the earlier decorations of that British basket-work which the Romans had learned to value and admire.

"The devices sculptured on a majority of the Scottish and Manx monoliths must have been executed before the artists possessed such skill or such tools as would enable them to cut the outline of the stone itself to any required form; they do not appear at that time to have set up crosses, but they engraved representations of that symbol on the surface of huge stones, many of which were already fixed in an erect position, and most probably had been for a long series of years employed in the services of an earlier religion. Upon such stones they imitated the ornamentation of wicker-work by innumerable reiterated blows of their small celts of flint, bronze, or iron, working out the design in low relief, and showing one-half of the round, or as much only of the osier wands as could be seen when plaited together. It is only in the later examples that the outline of the stone assumes the form of the cross; and this change is accompanied by a considerable alteration in the ornamental details, the interlacings become less elegant but more complicated, and terminate in the heads, tails, and limbs of various animals, often grotesque in expression; or, the wands burst into buds and leaves, or give place entirely to sculptured representations of men and animals of the rudest execution. It is a curious proof of the earlier use of the interwoven ornamentation, that it may be found in elegantly arranged and highly-finished devices on the same stones, with representations of the human figure so rudely carved as to appear to be the work of mere children.   .   .   .

"I have made careful copies of very numerous examples of ancient interlaced ornaments, and placed them in the hands of various artizans, particularly basket-makers, straw-plaiters, wire workers, and plaiters of ornamental hair.   They all inform me that, with a few exceptions, the devices may be worked out in their respective materials, and several thanked me for putting new patterns before them, which they said would be useful in their business.   Some of these drawings I gave to my own workpeople, who reproduced the devices very effectively in braid-work and embroidery.   They tell me they could, with time and patience, copy many of the most elaborate devices.   I must guard myself, however, against being supposed to assert that *all* the interlaced devices found on the old crosses may be reproduced in modern plait work; such is not the case.   Many of them may claim some other and very different origin, and there are others which the sculptor has doubtless modified and altered."

So much for the very probable origin of the characteristic school of intricate Interlaced Ornamentation, which we find in such perfection not only on sculptured stones, but in the elaborate illuminations of the earliest manuscripts executed in Ireland and the north of England.   On our two Plates of Celtic Interlaced Ornament are given a series of the more characteristic examples, which clearly show the great skill of our ancient artists in this class of design.   In some manuscripts, and notably the Book of Kells, preserved in the Library of Trinity College, Dublin, they are met with not only in the greatest profusion, but executed with a minuteness and accuracy perfectly marvellous.   We may now direct attention to the art works of the other nations which present examples of Interlaced Ornament.

Neither the Egyptians nor Greeks appear to have adopted interlaced patterns to any extent, though some of the diaper designs of the former, as the two upper examples on Plate Diaper Ornament, Egyptian [A]; and certain fret patterns of the latter, as Fig. 4, on Plate Fret Ornament, Egyptian and Classic, and Figs. 4 and 11, on Plate Fret Ornament, Classic [A], show the principles of interlaced ornamentation in their formation.   Probably one of the most notable examples of Greek origin is the pattern sculptured on the lower torus of the base of the Ionic order of the temple

6.

Minerva Polias, at Athens, which may be developed as shown in the accompanying cut, Fig. 6.   Other examples exist, all of which bear evidences of being suggested by plaited hair-work.

Next to the ancient Celtic artists, the Arabian and Moorish designers have displayed the greatest skill in Interlaced Ornament.   In their hands it assumed an angular and more strictly geometrical formation; the Celtic artists almost invariably introducing curved forms in their patterns, after the fashion of wicker-work. A comparison between the patterns on our Plates of Celtic and Moresque Interlaced Ornament will bring home clearly to the student the different principles of formation observed by these widely separated races of artists. The Moorish and Arabian designers carried their geometrical interlaced patterns, in the form of diapers, over large surfaces of walls and ceilings with the best possible effect.

In Byzantine and Gothic art, we find Interlaced Ornament sparingly used, except in the pages of certain illuminated manuscripts. We give a highly characteristic series of examples from Russian manuscripts, of Byzantine parentage, dating from the fourth to the fifteenth century. The difference of style is not very marked at any period in these examples. In Romanesque and Gothic architecture interlaced enrichments are not very common, nor are they met with to any extent in the remains of painted decoration. An early and simple example, in the form of a diaper, is to be seen on the spandrils of the nave arcades of Bayeux cathedral; here the design is evidently copied from simple basket-work. In Anglo-Norman work, especially in fonts, good examples are to be found, as in those of the churches of St. Mary, Stoke Cannon, Devon; St. Augustine, Locking, Somerset; St. Anne, Lewes, Sussex; and St. Leonard, Stanton Fitzwarren, Wilts.

POWDERED ORNAMENT

Powdered Ornament was used by the Egyptian artists, and, as might reasonably be expected, its first examples were in imitation of the sky at night—a deep blue ground, with yellow stars sprinkled over it. This decoration was freely used for ceilings. Other varieties of powderings were occasionally used for the ornamentation of uniform surfaces. The Assyrians and Babylonians were also familiar with this class of decoration, and probably employed it largely for their ceilings, but the total destruction of the upper portions of all their buildings leaves this an undecided question. We find a powdering of small rosettes on the dress of a king, in one of the sculptures of Khorsabad, which clearly proves that the Assyrians knew how to use the ornament with effect. The Greeks, doubtless, employed Powdered Ornament; its capacity for quiet and refined treatment must certainly have recommended it to their cultivated taste; but the Romans, and after them the Byzantine artists, do not appear to have much affected this simple class of ornamentation, delighting rather in designs in which flowing lines and scroll-work formed the more conspicuous features.

During the middle ages, when richly embroidered and woven fabrics were largely used for dresses, hangings, etc., Powdered Ornament came to be freely used. In imitation of these fabrics, it appeared on the vaults and walls of ecclesiastical buildings, assuming the forms of symbolical and heraldic devices, monograms, crosses, and the like. Probably the two most commonly used devices, in France at least, were the fleur-de-lys and five-pointed star, the former both symbolical and heraldic, and the latter in imitation of the stars of heaven. Both were commonly executed in gold or yellow upon deep blue

7.

8.

grounds. These powderings are given in the accompanying cuts, Figs. 7 and 8. Numerous illustrations of the use of Powdered Ornament are to be found in the miniatures of the manuscripts of the fourteenth and fifteenth centuries. Words, sometimes inscribed on small ribbons or scrolls, were frequently used as powderings by middle age artists. A characteristic example of this treatment is to be seen on the brass of Sir John de Brewys, in Wiston Church, Sussex. The powderings in this case consist of the words 𝕵𝖊𝖘𝖚𝖘 and 𝖒𝖊𝖗𝖈𝖞, on small scrolls, placed diagonally. Illustrations of powderings, in the mediæval style, are given in Plate POWDERED ORNAMENT, MODERN FRENCH, taken from the decorations of the lateral chapels of the cathedral of Notre-Dame, at Paris, designed by the late M. Viollet-le-Duc. They are all more or less of an emblematic character.

In Arabian and Moresque art, Powdered Ornament is never met with in its pure form, and indeed rarely in any form. In Persian art, however, it is very common, and generally beautifully treated in the shape of sprigs of conventional flowers and foliage. The carpets and other textile fabrics, for which Persia has been famed from the earliest times, display a great variety of Powdered Ornaments. The artists of other Oriental nations—India, China, and Japan—are all well acquainted with this class of decoration, and use it freely in all departments of their works. The Japanese, however, display the greatest originality and freedom in their treatment of powderings, and, unlike all other artists, frequently break through all rules of uniformity and regularity of disposition. The leading varieties of Japanese Powdered Ornamentation are given on the four Plates, POWDERED ORNAMENT, JAPANESE [A] [B] and [C], and POWDERED DIAPER ORNAMENT, JAPANESE. In the ten designs given it will be observed that a regular disposition of the devices is the exception, and an irregular disposition the rule. There is no question that the latter treatment, in the hands of such skilful artists as the Japanese, is attended with most charming results. The styles of Powdered Ornament represented by the lower designs on Plates [B] and [C] are great favourites with the native artists, and are extremely crisp and effective. It is obvious that in such styles it is not necessary to have any two devices exactly alike, and this is a great advantage when the decoration is executed by hand with the free brush; all that has to be studied is an equal weight of pattern and space in all parts, so that the general effect may be uniform to the eye. In Middle Age decorative art, irregular powderings of stars were occasionally introduced, in direct imitation of the starry heavens; and such a treatment is far more artistic than the regular disposition of stars of one size, as in Fig. 7. In such powderings, not only should the stars be placed erratically, but they should vary in size and number of points, say five, seven, and nine, for odd numbers invariably are most pleasing.

DIAPER ORNAMENT

Of all classes of decorative ornament, that designated Diaper Ornament is the most varied in design and widely spread in its adoption. Most nations who have achieved any skill in ornamental art have shown their greatest ingenuity in the formation and treatment of diapers. Diaper Ornament may be generally defined as that species of design in which certain leading features or devices occur at regular intervals, and which are enclosed or connected by geometrical or flowing lines, sometimes independent and at others forming integral portions of the devices. Examples of all the more important classes of Diaper Ornament are given in our series of Plates. The class based on fret patterns has already been alluded to.

Representative examples of Egyptian origin are given on Plates DIAPER ORNAMENT, EGYPTIAN [A] and [B]. Besides such as these, the Egyptian artists used designs in which the lotus and papyrus flowers were introduced in their usual conventional types. The flowers were commonly connected or enclosed by curved and spiral lines. Of the numerous simple geometrical diapers derived from woven fabrics and bead-work it is unnecessary to speak.

The Assyrian artists apparently used Diaper Ornament freely; but owing to the limited number of examples preserved to us on their sculptures, we can form only an imperfect idea of their skill in this direction. Those which exist are mostly of a formal or geometrical character, such as rosettes enclosed within squares, and of little suggestive value to the ornamentist of to-day.

In the construction of diapers of a strictly geometrical character, no designers have surpassed the Arabian and Moorish. We give four examples on Plate ARABIAN, of severe geometrical diapers, which are highly characteristic of Arabian art. The principles on which these are formed are very evident and require no particular comment. Turning our attention to Moresque ornament, we find one of the most ingenious and remarkable schools of diaper design which exists in the entire range of decorative art. One example, quite sufficient for the main purpose of the present Work, is given on Plate MORESQUE. It is taken from that epitome of Moorish art, the Alhambra. Speaking of the principles on which the Moorish artists constructed their beautiful and elaborate patterns, Owen Jones remarks :—" Their general forms were first cared for; these were subdivided by general lines; the interstices were then filled in with ornament, which was again subdivided and enriched for closer inspection. They carried out this principle with the greatest refinement, and the harmony and beauty of all their ornamentation derive their chief success from its observance. Their main divisions contrast admirably and balance; the greatest distinctness is obtained; the detail never interferes with the general form : when seen at a distance, the main lines strike the eye; as we approach nearer, the detail comes into the composition; on a closer inspection, we see still further detail on the surface of the ornaments themselves. . . . A still further charm is found in the works of the Arabs and Moors from their conventional treatment of ornament, which, forbidden as they were by their creed to represent living forms, they carried to the highest perfection. They ever worked as nature worked, but always avoided a direct transcript; they took her principles, but did not, as we do, attempt to copy her works. In this they do not stand alone; in every period of faith in art, all ornamentation was ennobled by the ideal; never was the sense of propriety violated by a too faithful representation of nature. . . . Whether the Moors in their marvellous decorations worked on certain fixed rules, or only in accordance with a highly-organised natural instinct to which they had arrived by centuries of refinement upon the works of their predecessors, it would be difficult to say. One person may sing in tune by natural instinct, as another may by acquired knowledge. The happier state, however, is where *knowledge ministers to instinct;* and we are inclined to believe that this must have been the case with the Moors. If the poet tells us to study their *works with attention*, and promises us a reward of a commentary on decoration, does it not imply that there was in them something that might be *learned*, as well as much that might be *felt*? If it had been the latter only, the poet would have said, 'Come and enjoy,' not 'Come and study.'"

On Plates PERSIAN [A] and [B] are given four designs from beautiful enamelled wall tiles. These show the peculiar treatment of Diaper Ornament followed by the Persian and Arabo-Persian artists in their best decorative works. Their method of arranging and conventionalising the natural forms is most ingenious and artistic; and the freedom and grace imparted to all the lines are well deserving of careful study and imitation by the designer of to-day.

Little need be said of the series of Japanese Diapers given on our five Plates, further than that the designs have been carefully selected to represent the entire scope of Japanese art in this direction. All are highly suggestive.

In Gothic art, Diaper Ornament appears in the greatest profusion. It is met with in architectural sculpture, occasionally covering large wall spaces, as in the spandrils of the main arcades and triforium at Westminster abbey; it frequently occurs in illuminations of manuscripts, stained glass, embroidery, tiles, metal work, wood carving and woven fabrics; and is largely used, in one style or another, for mural painted decoration. In all these forms it is replete with suggestiveness to the modern designer. In our series of Plates devoted to mediæval examples, derived from mural paintings, mosaic work, and textile fabrics, the leading types of treatment will be found. The four designs on Plate ENGLISH MIDDLE AGE [A] are from paintings between the clerestory windows of the church of West Walton, Norfolk. Patterns 1, 2, and 3 are executed in a quiet-toned red on a buff ground. Pattern 4 is also in red, with the addition of blue in the circles on the light bands. The architecture is of the Early English period; and the paintings are in all likelihood contemporaneous. The following Plate, SICILIAN [A], shows four designs almost as severe in treatment as the preceding. They are from the mosaics of the cathedral of Monreale, near Palermo, and are of thirteenth century work, and accordingly of about the same date as the English examples. The two Plates just alluded to, along with Plates MIDDLE AGE [D] and [H], practically cover the entire range of mediæval geometrical Diaper Ornament, so far at least as general treatment and disposition of parts are concerned. The designs on the latter Plate are from the walls of the upper church of St. Francesco, at Assisi: they are of late thirteenth century workmanship, and probably designed by Cimabue.

We come now to a class of Diaper Ornament largely used in embroidery, textile fabrics, and, in imitation of these, for mural decoration. The four Plates, DUTCH MIDDLE AGE [A] [A*] [B] and [C], are from decorative paintings in the church of St. Bavon, at Haarlem. They occur in oblong pieces, are surrounded by narrow borders, and have a fringe along their lower edges; this treatment clearly shows their origin, for they simply represent the costly hangings and cloths of estate so frequently hung in churches and mansions during the middle ages. These designs appear to have been painted during the first decade of the sixteenth century Diapers of this class are of great variety, and admit of endless modifications according to the ingenuity and taste of the designer. They may be constructed on curved or sweeping lines of any form; and with any type of leaf, flower, or fruit, more or less severely conventionalised. They are invaluable for the decoration of large surfaces, and when executed in quiet tones of colour produce a most agreeable and refined effect. They are probably the most beautiful and appropriate class of designs for woven fabrics suitable for curtains, hangings, &c.; and when produced about the scale of our illustrations, in suitable materials, form admirable coverings for furniture. The methods of colouring adopted in the originals, in the church of St. Bavon, are noted on the Plates.

On Plates MIDDLE AGE [E] [F] and [G] are given four examples of other styles of Diaper Ornament, also derived from textile fabrics. Their value and suggestiveness to the decorative artist are at once apparent. The design on Plate [E] is from a fifteenth century velvet in South Kensington Museum; it is a good specimen of a style much in vogue during the fourteenth and fifteenth centuries. There is a vast field for the ingenious designer in diapers of this type, and such flowers as the rose, lily, passion-flower, chrysanthemum, aster, and thistle; such leaves as those of the vine, ivy, sycamore, horse-chesnut, and wood-sorrel; and such fruit as the pine-apple, pomegranate, and grape, all of course strictly conventionalised, lend themselves freely to his adaptation. For ecclesiastical or heraldic purposes, symbols, monograms, badges, or other devices may occupy a central position in either the leading or subordinate divisions of the designs. While great freedom is given to the designer in this description of diaper, he must strive in all cases to secure a uniform distribution of detail and an even effect of colour. Like the diaper ornamentation of the Moors, his patterns should charm the eye when viewed at a distance, and gratify the artistic sense when seen in detail. On Plates [F] and [G] are diaper patterns in a style which was much in favour during the fourteenth century, and which appears to have originated in Sicily, where it was probably founded on Eastern motives. The Italian looms of the fourteenth and early part of the fifteenth century produced magnificent fabrics of silk and gold, with patterns in this style. The two designs on Plate [F] are from specimens in South Kensington Museum, and appear to be of Italian workmanship, probably the product of the celebrated Lucca looms. All are highly suggestive, and may be studied by the modern designer with advantage.

We have considered it desirable to lay before the English decorative artist a representative series of designs taken from the important decorative works at the cathedral of Notre-Dame and the Sainte-Chapelle, at Paris; the abbey church of Saint-Denis; and the church of Notre-Dame de Bon-Secours, near Rouen. These decorations have been executed under the direction of the late M. Viollet-de-Duc and other able architects. The sixteen designs given on Plates DIAPER ORNAMENT, MODERN FRENCH [A] to [G], represent all the leading varieties of treatment met with in these works, and are full of suggestions to the designer of Gothic Diaper Ornament. The schemes of the colouring are given as guides; but it must have been observed by all who have seen the decorations at the Sainte-Chapelle, the abbey of Saint-Denis, and the church at Rouen, that the tones of the colours adopted by the French artists are far too powerful and crude. The paintings, by M. Viollet-de-Duc, in the chapels of Notre-Dame, are, however, much more subdued and refined in tone. On Plate [G] are given two diapers from these chapels. The paintings at the Sainte-Chapelle, by M. Duban, are stated to be restorations of thirteenth century work; to what extent they are accurate reproductions it is not easy to decide. Two designs from this elaborately decorated building are given on Plate [E]. On Plates [C] and [D] are four diapers from columns in the chevet and Lady chapel of the abbey of Saint-Denis. The other Plates contain designs from the church of Notre-Dame de Bon-Secours.

CONVENTIONAL FOLIAGE

On the Plates containing examples of different styles of Conventional Foliage will be found much to help the modern designer and practical decorator; to the latter the series of Greek patterns will be most useful in the development of borders, bands, and such like decorations. On Plates MIDDLE AGE [A] [B] and [C] are given examples of the most suggestive types of foliage from the pages of illuminated manuscripts. Plate [A] contains specimens from the tenth century *Benedictional of St. Æthelwold.* Figs. 1 and 2, on Plate [B], are of twelfth century date; Figs. 3, 4, and 5 are of the fifteenth century. Fig. 1, on Plate [C], is from a fourteenth century manuscript; and the remaining examples are of fifteenth century design.

On Plates MODERN FRENCH [A] [C] and [D] are given numerous examples of Conventional Foliage from the paintings of the chapels of Notre-Dame, at Paris, designed by M. Viollet-le-Duc. These, we feel assured, will often be referred to by the ornamentist.

In conclusion, we may acknowledge we have found considerable difficulty in selecting materials for our present Work. We have alone been guided by the desire to introduce nothing but what would prove of every-day value to the designer and practical decorator.   How far we have been successful others must decide.   We feel certain, however, if the student of ornamental art will only learn all that our Plates can teach him, he will not have very much more to master to render him perfectly at home in general matters of form and arrangement, so far as surface ornamentation is concerned.

FRET ORNAMENT

PLATE 1
FRET ORNAMENT.   EGYPTIAN AND CLASSIC.

2

3

1

4

5

6

7

PLATE 2
FRET ORNAMENT.   CLASSIC [A].

3

4

5

6

2

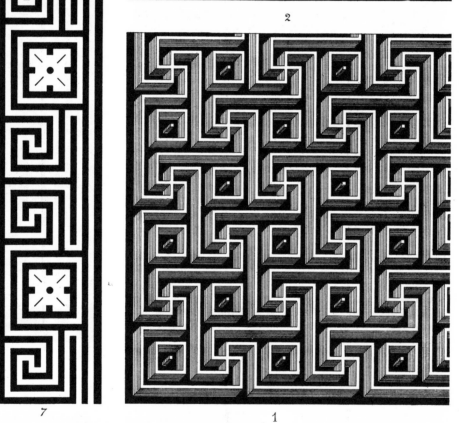

7

1

8

9

10

11

12

W. J. A., DEL.

PLATE 3
FRET ORNAMENT.

MIDDLE AGE [A].

3

4

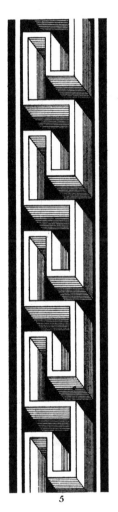

5

2

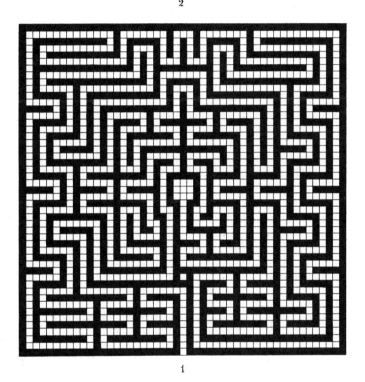

1

6

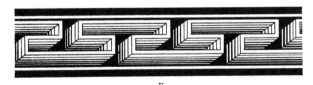

7

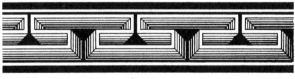

8

9

10

W. J. A., DEL.

PLATE 4
FRET ORNAMENT.   ORIENTAL [A].

S. R. A., DEL.

PLATE 5
FRET DIAPER ORNAMENT.   JAPANESE.

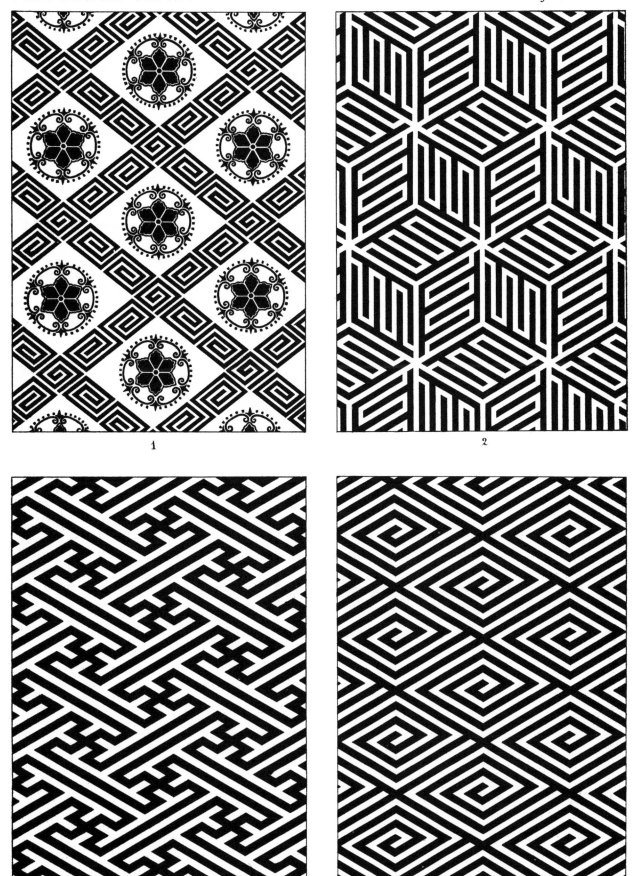

1

2

3

4

INTERLACED ORNAMENT

PLATE 6
INTERLACED ORNAMENT.

CELTIC.

S. R. A., DEL.

PLATE 7
INTERLACED ORNAMENT.   CELTIC [B].

S. R. A., DEL.

PLATE 8
INTERLACED ORNAMENT.   ARABIAN.

S. R. A. & G. W. DEL.

PLATE 9
INTERLACED ORNAMENT.

MORESQUE.

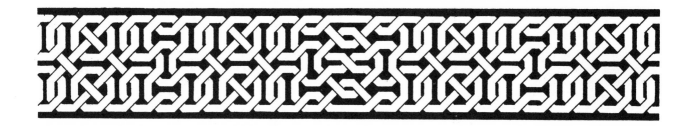

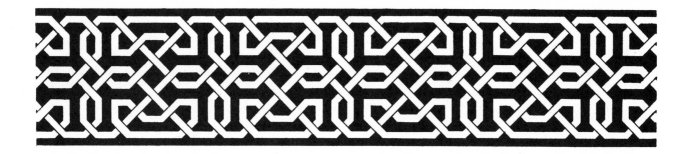

PLATE 10
INTERLACED ORNAMENT.

MORESQUE [B].

S. R. A. & G. W. DEL.

PLATE 11
INTERLACED ORNAMENT

MIDDLE AGE [A].

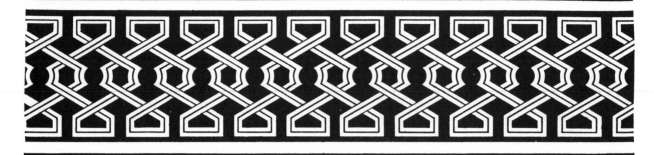

S. R. A., F. S., & G. W., DEL.

PLATE 12
INTERLACED ORNAMENT.   RUSSIAN MIDDLE AGE.

POWDERED ORNAMENT

PLATE 13
POWDERED DIAPER ORNAMENT

JAPANESE

S. R. A., DEL

1

2

PLATE 14
POWDERED ORNAMENT.

S. R. A., DEL.

PLATE 15
POWDERED ORNAMENT.

JAPANESE [A].

S. R. A. DEL

PLATE 16
POWDERED ORNAMENT

JAPANESE [B]

S. R. A., DEL.

PLATE 17
POWDERED ORNAMENT   JAPANESE [C].

DIAPER ORNAMENT

PLATE 18
DIAPER ORNAMENT,   EGYPTIAN [A].

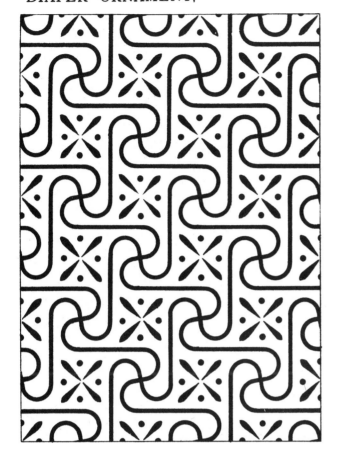

PLATE 19
DIAPER ORNAMENT.

EGYPTIAN [B].

1

2

3

4

S. R. A., DEL.

PLATE 20
DIAPER ORNAMENT

ARABIAN.

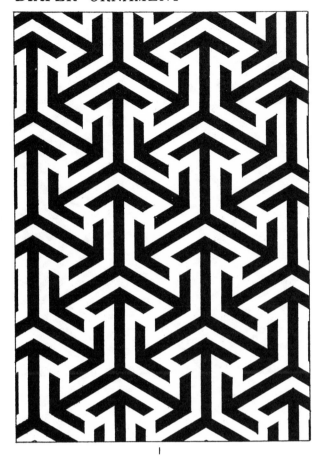

1

2

3

4

G. A. A., DEL.

PLATE 21
DIAPER ORNAMENT.   MORESQUE.

S. R. A., DEL.

PLATE 22
DIAPER ORNAMENT

S. R. A., DEL.

PLATE 23
DIAPER ORNAMENT.

PERSIAN [B]

PLATE 24
DIAPER ORNAMENT.

JAPANESE [A].

1

2

3

4

S. R. A. DEL.

PLATE 25
DIAPER ORNAMENT.   JAPANESE [B].

1

2

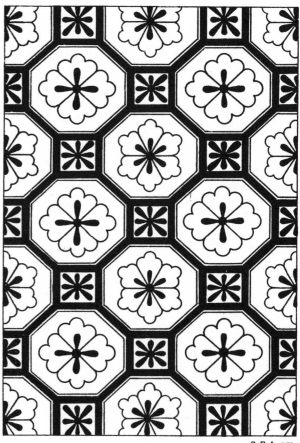

3   4   S. R. A. DEL.

PLATE 26

DIAPER ORNAMENT

JAPANESE [C].

S. R. A., DEL

2

1

PLATE 27
DIAPER ORNAMENT,

JAPANESE [D].

1

2

3

4

S. R. A., DEL.

PLATE 28
DIAPER ORNAMENT,
JAPANESE [E].

1

2

3

4

S. R. A., DEL.

PLATE 29
DIAPER ORNAMENT

ENGLISH MIDDLE AGE [A].

1

2

3

4

S. R. A., DEL

PLATE 30
DIAPER ORNAMENT.   SICILIAN [A].

1

2

3

4

S. R. A., DEL.

PLATE 31
DIAPER ORNAMENT

DUTCH MIDDLE AGE [A].

A Green—B Red—C Gold—Main Outlines in Black; the Inner Lines in Red and Green.

S. R. A. DEL.

PLATE 32
DIAPER ORNAMENT   DUTCH MIDDLE AGE [A].

A Green—B Gold—C Red—All Outlined in Black.

S. R. A., DEL

PLATE 33
DIAPER ORNAMENT.

DUTCH MIDDLE AGE [B].

A *Deep Orange—B Brown—Ornament in Gold, Outlined with Brown.*

S. R. A., DEL.

PLATE 34
DIAPER ORNAMENT

DUTCH MIDDLE AGE [C].

A Crimson Ground—B Blue—C Gold—Outlined with Black.

S. R. A., DEL.

PLATE 35
DIAPER ORNAMENT.

MODERN FRENCH [A].

Green Ground—Pattern in Gold, Outlined with Black.

Scarlet Ground—A White—B Green—C Gold—Outlined with Black.

S. R. A. DEL.

PLATE 36
DIAPER ORNAMENT.

MODERN FRENCH [B].

Green Ground—A White—B Gold—Outlined with Black.

S. R. A del.

Green Ground—Pattern in Gold, Outlined with Black.

PLATE 37
DIAPER ORNAMENT

MODERN FRENCH [B]

Red Ground—Pattern in Gold—Outlined with Black.

Green Ground—Pattern in Gold—Outlined with Black.

S. R. A., DEL.

PLATE 38
DIAPER ORNAMENT

MODERN FRENCH [C].

H. P. & G. W., DEL.

A White, B Gold, C Blue, D Green, Outlined with Black.

1.

2.

H. P. & G. W., DEL.

2.

PLATE 39
DIAPER ORNAMENT

A Buff, B Red, C Blue, D Green, E Yellow, Outlined with Black.

1.

W. J. A., DEL.

A Gold Ground—B Blue—C Red—Outlined with Black.

PLATE 40
DIAPER ORNAMENT.

A Gold Ground—B Blue—C Red—Outlined with Black.

PLATE 41
DIAPER ORNAMENT.

MODERN FRENCH [F].

Red Ground—Gold Ornament—Outlined with Black.   H. P.

Red Ground—Ornament Gold—Outlined with Black.   F. W S., DEL.

MODERN FRENCH [G.

S. R. A., DEL.

PLATE 42
DIAPER ORNAMENT

GERMAN MIDDLE AGE [A]

Gold and Green Counterchanged, Red beaks and feet.

S. R. A., DEL.

PLATE 43
DIAPER ORNAMENT

Gold upon Crimson Ground.

PLATE 44
DIAPER ORNAMENT

MIDDLE AGE [D].

1

2

3

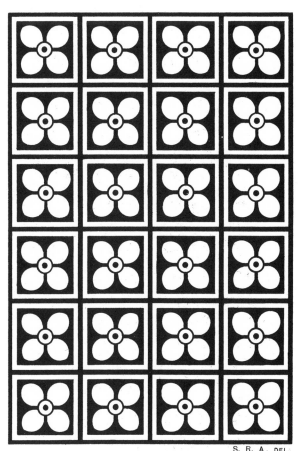

4

S. R. A., DEL

PLATE 45
DIAPER ORNAMENT.   MIDDLE AGE [E].

S. R. A., DEL.

2

PLATE 46
DIAPER ORNAMENT.

PLATE 47
DIAPER ORNAMENT.

MIDDLE AGE [G].

PLATE 48
DIAPER ORNAMENT

MIDDLE AGE [H].

CHINESE.

S. R. A., DEL.

PLATE 49
DIAPER ORNAMENT.

CONVENTIONAL FOLIAGE

PLATE 50
CONVENTIONAL FOLIAGE

MIDDLE AGE [A].

PLATE 51
CONVENTIONAL FOLIAGE.

MIDDLE AGE [B].

PLATE 52
CONVENTIONAL FOLIAGE.

MIDDLE AGE [C].

MODERN FRENCH [A].

PLATE 53
CONVENTIONAL FOLIAGE

PLATE 54
CONVENTIONAL FOLIAGE.

MODERN FRENCH [B].

Blue Grounds—Ornaments in Red, Yellow, Green, Brown and White—Outlined with Black.

PLATE 55
CONVENTIONAL FOLIAGE.   MODERN FRENCH [C].

PLATE 56
CONVENTIONAL FOLIAGE.

MODERN FRENCH [D]

S. R. A., DEL.

PLATE 57
CONVENTIONAL FOLIAGE.

PERSIAN.

PLATE 58
CONVENTIONAL FOLIAGE.

S. R. A. DEL.

PLATE 59
CONVENTIONAL FOLIAGE.

GREEK [B].

S. R. A., DEL.

PLATE 60
CONVENTIONAL FOLIAGE.

JAPANESE.

S. R. A., DEL.